Sorrento Travel Guide

Sightseeing, Hotel, Restaurant & Shopping Highlights

Katherine Higgins

Copyright © 2015, Astute Press
All Rights Reserved.

No part of this publication may be reproduced, stored in a retrieval system, or transmitted, in any form or by any means without the prior written permission of the publisher, nor be otherwise circulated in any form of binding or cover other than that in which it is published and without similar condition being imposed on the subsequent purchaser.

If there are any errors or omissions in copyright acknowledgements the publisher will be pleased to insert the appropriate acknowledgement in any subsequent printing of this publication.

Although we have taken all reasonable care in researching this book we make no warranty about the accuracy or completeness of its content and disclaim all liability arising from its use

Table of Contents

Sorrento 5
Culture 7
Location & Orientation 8
Climate & When to Visit 9

Sightseeing Highlights 10
Correale di Terranova Museum 10
Piazza Tasso 11
Cathedral of San Filippo & Giacomo 13
Small Marina/Large Marina 14
Baths of Regina Giovanna 15
Via del Capo (Panoramic View) 17
Amalfi Coast Day Trip 18
Pompeii Historical Site 19
Capri Island 21
Naples 23

Recommendations for the Budget Traveller 26
Places to Stay 26
Sorrento 26
Ravello (Amalfi Coast) 27
Pompeii 28
Naples 28
Places to Eat 29
Sant'anna da Emilia 29
Zi'Antonio 30
Taverna Azzura 30
Gelateria Davide 31
Places to Shop 31
Macramé 31
Limonoro 32
De Cenzo 32

SORRENTO TRAVEL GUIDE

Sorrento

The quaint Amalfi Coast town of Sorrento has beautiful architecture and a scenic main square with quaint cafes, restaurants and shops. Sorrento is on the Circumvesuviana rail line and can be quickly reached from Naples. It is also an ideal base for visiting Pompeii, Herculaneum and the island of Capri.

Walk to the top of the hills of Sorrento and look across the beautiful Bay of Naples. Squint your eyes, and look for Mount Vesuvius, one of the most famous and powerful volcanoes in history.

He's quiet, for now, but every now and then a rumble, or a cloud of steam rising from the peak, to remind those who live in his shadow that he's still there. To remind yourself of the power of this massive living mountain, take a trip to Pompeii, (just a short train ride from Sorrento) and see the results of the powerful eruption that buried the town and its people for millennia.

But for now, climb back down that hill, into the sun-warmed streets of Sorrento, into the pinks and blues and coral and green, and bask in the Mediterranean food and culture that has made Sorrento a much-loved tourist city.

The oldest ruins in Sorrento date back to over three millennia ago. It was an important town for the Romans, as gorges that run a ring around the city made it easily defendable, then even after the fall of the Roman Empire, it switched sides to be placed under the control of the Byzantines, then back to Napoli, then finally to the new Italian Kingdom in 1861. Now, Sorrento is an extremely popular tourist destination that was a favorite of both Goethe and Keats.

Here you will find colorful discotheques throbbing late into the night, balanced with the sleepy afternoons of a siesta culture. Here you will find the delicious liquor limoncello, made fresh here for centuries. Here you will find shopping, and wine, and swimming in some of the most beautiful waters known to man.

Sorrento is an area of the world that has been occupied for almost as long as humans have walked upright. Go find out why.

Culture

Italia, Italia, there's no culture quite like there is there. Everything is said with a mixture of beautifully articulated speech and gestures, hands to the side, palms up with a question, shoulders shrugged way up to say "I don't know." What you do know in Italy, however, is that you will be fed, you will be taken care of, you will be given heaps and heaps of seconds and thirds, and all your senses will be satiated, smells, sounds, sights, until you close your eyes for the evening and open them again the next day to church bells ringing, and Vespas buzzing along the street.

Buon giorno says "good morning", and a smile says it all. Sorrento has been a haven for tourists and sailors for millennia, so it is safe to say that the residents here are used to wide-eyed visitors, and stuttering attempts at the local language. Even if buon giorno is all you can muster, that should be enough, and you'll find the local population helpful and generous.

Sorrento is in the south of Italy, which is remarkably different than its northern counterpoint. There are some theorists that say that Italy was never truly unified, that the North and the South remain as different as ever they were. Don't expect the hustle and bustle of the more commercial Milan, or the towering cultural monuments of Rome and Florence. Sorrento prides itself in being a coastal gem, a sometimes-quiet, sometimes-rowdy southern sister of the Italian cities, and caters to tourists from all over the world.

Expect local pizza and pastas, and fresh fish and local wines. Also expect restaurants who tailor to the hoards of visitors who descend upon Sorrento each year – wiener schnitzel to the German tourists, and noodles for the Japanese. Don't expect to have this city to yourself; its secret was leaked too long ago to fathom, but do your homework before you go to ensure that your time in Sorrento and the surrounding countryside is everything you wanted from your Italian holiday.

Location & Orientation

Sorrento is located in the south of Italy, a short train ride from Pompeii or Naples. It also has access to several of the smaller islands off the coast of Italy, such as Capri, and you can find that it's easy to reach Sorrento by car, bus, train, or boat. If you are flying, you want to take a flight to Naples Capodichino Airport, then take either a car, bus, or train from Naples to Sorrento.

You may find the train to be the most accessible, as this is what most Italians use to visit the area. You want to take the Circumvesuviana (around Vesuvius) train, which departs most days every 30 minutes and will take you about 2 hours to arrive. The cost will be about 4 Euros, so you will have plenty of money left over for a glass of wine as your train winds its way to the coast.

Climate & When to Visit

Sorrento is on the Mediterranean coast, and has a temperate climate. That said, it gets quite hot in the summer months, in July and August, which also seems to be when the majority of Northern European visitors descend upon this coastal town.

Before you visit, think about what you'd like to do when you get here. If your idea of a perfect Italian vacation is beaches, late-night discos, crowded streets, and restaurants that are open for business until the small hours of the night, you'd probably like to visit from April – August, when most of the visitors are in Sorrento, and most companies and businesses catering to the tourism trade are open and fully operational.

If you'd like a calmer, perhaps a bit chillier sojourn in Sorrento, feel free to come in the winter months. You'll be just fine with a light jacket and long trousers, and you'll have a lot of restaurants to yourself, but just be prepared for transportation options to be reduced somewhat, and some stores closed. Sorrento has a marvelous tourism website that you should check before you're thinking about visiting:
http://www.sorrentotourism.com/en/index.php.

When calling the numbers below, keep in mind that the country code for Italy is +39.

Sightseeing Highlights

Correale di Terranova Museum

The 1700's was a century of pleasure and enjoyment for those who could afford it. Wigs were powdered, corsets tied tight, paintings small and intricate, necessitating a long gaze to appreciate their beauty. Take a dive into this century in this museum, which contains dozens of beautiful examples of paintings, miniatures, and porcelains to be appreciated over a long, lazy morning during your visit to Sorrento.

A wonderful place to start in your exploration of Sorrento has to be this museum, built in the 1700's on land given to the Correale family from the Queen of Aragon in 1498. It is special for so many reasons, but particularly for the collection of Neapolitan art and also the vista its land offers. From the land, you can look over and have a beautiful view of the panoramic Sorrento coast. For a first look, this is one not to miss.

The museum holds some odd hours, so it is a good idea to check the website below before you visit. Normally, it is open Wednesday through Monday from 9:30 am to 1:30, April through September. On Wednesdays and Saturdays the museum has extended hours, which may be that perfect chance to enjoy a rich, beautiful sunset from the view from the esplanade at the museum.

Address: Via Correale 50, Sorrento, 80067
Telephone 081 8781846
www.museocorreale.it

Piazza Tasso

Everyone can tell you that the piazza is the place to be, when the sun is set, and bellies are full from a delightful Italian meal, when the guitar players dust off their picks, and young artists paint their faces gold or silver or white, feigning to be statues that move when you drop a coin in their hat. It's a place to see and be seen, to listen and to sing if the spirit moves you. This is Italy, after all. Music is the mortar between the stones in every building, and with wine this cheap, you'll find yourself singing along to just about anything.

Piazza Tasso is the largest and main square of Sorrento. Inside the piazza, you can find the Cathedral of Carmine, which is open to visitors if you need a quick moment of solitude after the hustle and bustle of the piazza.

During the day, this piazza is busy with traffic, both car and pedestrian, but in the evening the piazza takes on a life of its own as police limit the amount of traffic coming through the piazza. You'll find residents here relaxing after a day of work, and enjoy a cup of coffee or glass of vino (wine) as you people-watch yourself to nirvana.

Once you've had your fill of people watching and imbibing, take a walk down Via San Cesareo, which is a busy shopping street, and carries a huge assortment of the lemon liquors and sweets that Sorrento is known for. Here you will have to try some limoncello, a liquor made of lemon zest and peel. It is sweet and sharp, and is a perfect digestive for any night on your sojourn.

Address: Corso Italia, Sorrento

Cathedral of San Filippo & Giacomo

Take a walk through the small twists and turns of the ancient city of Sorrento, and you're bound to wind up at the Duomo, or main cathedral, of the city. It is strange to think that this relatively small and understated structure is the city's most prominent religious meeting places, and has been for centuries now. But step inside, into the dim and humid interior, and you can still hear the echo of the choirs that have sung there, the tears of widows and smiles of brides, and bells ringing to harken the faithful to prayer.

You can find the Duomo on the Corso Italia, and at first its simple yet bright façade may confuse you, and you will check your map to make sure you've actually arrived at the right location. The first thing you will see is its beautiful façade; it is a surprisingly cheery yellow color, with columns as cross-sections and various sculptures dotting each side, a mark of the architecture of Borromini, a well-known architect of the time. It is unmistakably from the renaissance, and is a must on your visit to Sorrento. But step inside, and immediately the opulence you find will take you aback. You can find frescoes painted on the walls by local artists from Naples, and also a carved rendition of the Crucifixion underneath a sumptuous arch.

In the beautiful and sun-speckled interior, you can find that all surfaces, from the walls, to the floor, to the soaring ceiling above, are covered in color, inlaid wood and stone, and glass in every color imaginable. Smell the incense used during Sunday mass, used for centuries now, and creates a thick, sweet interior even on days it is not used.

The choir lofts were rebuilt in the last few centuries, and show remarkable craftsmanship and integration into the original building.

If you are there to visit, or take place in the masses that are still held in this 15th century treasure, make sure you take a shawl or cardigan, as bare shoulders are frowned upon in this sacred space.

Adddress: Largo Arcivescovado: At the corner of Corso Italia and Via. R.R. Giuliani, Sorrento

Ask at your hotel for visiting hours and time of mass.

Small Marina/Large Marina

No trip to the south of Italy, particularly in the sticky summer months, is complete without a trip to the beach. Don't expect sprawling white sparkling sand here – these beaches are located right in the city itself, and function as marinas as well as a gathering place for sun-worshippers and children splashing in and out of the water.

Because of the topography of the coastline around Sorrento, finding a beach without having to scale a cliff can be a difficult thing to do. Lucky for us Sorrento have Marina Piccola (Small Marina) and Marina Grande (Big Marina) right smack in the middle of town with beautiful beaches to visit.

Marina Piccola can be found from following Via Marina Piccola straight from Piazza Tasso, which makes it incredibly convenient. You can also find boats here that will take you on coastal excursions.

Marina Grande can be found extremely close to the Piazza della Vittoria, and is, as you can tell from the name, the larger of the two options. In fact, Marina Grande actually looks and feels like a small fishing village, and you can easily spend all day between lounging on the beach, renting a jet ski or motorboat, then wandering to the sea-facing street, choosing between the pastel-colored buildings for a bite to eat. There is no car traffic in this area, and you can drift a few centuries in the past easily during a long quiet day here.

It is an easy walk out to either Marina Piccola or Marina Grande, just ask the information desk at your hotel or hostel for directions. Wear your walking shoes; it can be a steep descent down to the Marinas, and a steep walk back, but not long at all, as the city of Sorrento is so compact.

Baths of Regina Giovanna

After a few days' basking in the noises and salty air of Sorrento, you may want to strap on some walking shoes and take a look around the gorgeous countryside around you. Sorrento is an excellent starting point for excursions both on land and by foot, and it's safe to say that boredom just isn't an option during this trip.

Legend has it that in the early 14th century, Regina Giovanna, the Queen of Naples, would come here to bathe, far away from peeping Toms. Legend further has it that she would do much more here than just bathe, history having painted her a somewhat lustful color, but one look at the baths she would visit will still even the most torrid of stories, and you can relax in the crisp, cool water in which history is so deeply soaked.

The baths are an easy trip. You take a bus to the city bus terminus, and take a small path that begins there, at the Cape of Sorrento. You can feel free to follow other tourists, or locals that look out to take a walk, as this is a popular spot for relaxation. Take a small walk, and then a climb down a steep staircase, and you will reach a beautiful lagoon, filled with clear blue water, and illuminated by the sun above. Feel free to take a dip, and wade under the natural arch that soars above the hidden lagoon. This is indeed a magical place, and floating in the cool waters, you can imagine what stories were made here, this place so conducive to secrecy and love.

There is also the ruins of a magnificent Roman villa here, built during the first century, that you can explore freely, and a larger, somewhat rocky beach that you can stretch out on after your trip to the baths.

To get here, take the bus to the Cape of Sorrento, or take the SITA bus to Massalubrense.

Via del Capo (Panoramic View)

A trip to Sorrento is certainly not complete without taking in – breathlessly – the magnificent vistas from the Via del Capo. This is best to do on a cool afternoon, when the sun is lower and the heat of the day has relatively passed you by. Step onto the Corso Italia, and go west until you can see that the street changes its name to Via del Capo. You will find yourself travelling away from the center of town, away from the hustle and bustle of traffic and car horns.

Here you will pass by some of the more expensive hotels, and also some tiny beaches. Take a pause and dip your feet in the cool water. This will rejuvenate you for the rest of your walk.

If you want to pause for dinner, stop at Marina Puolo, with its restaurants, cafés, and small, creaking fishing boats. Pass by an ancient Roman villa, now ruined, using a just as ancient rocky path.

Along your walk, look around you, out over the Bay of Naples. Look at the boats coming in from a long day of fishing, and the Bay changing color with the falling sun. You can also look back and see the view towards the Cape (Capo), and those gorgeous white limestone cliffs that will also change color and morph with the passing of the day.

Stop in a small restaurant on your way back, or sit on a beach and watch the sun set. Walking up the Via del Capo is a perfect way to end a perfect day in Italy.

Amalfi Coast Day Trip

Taking a day trip along the Amalfi Coast is an exercise in faith. You may find yourself holding your breath as the driver whips back and forth at the edge of the cliffs that extend out of Sorrento. Breathe in, hold in your breath, and let it out slowly. The driver is in control, and you are in for a journey like no other as the trip takes you up and out of Sorrento, and along some of the most beautiful strips of land known to man. It's no wonder they say mermaids used to occupy these waters, and princes and kings and adventurers alike would attempt to land on these opulent shores.

You will find that the driver or company you choose for your day tour is very flexible: if you are more interested in sampling local Italian fare, then you will find a good part of your day is spent in the local markets or even a hidden restaurant hanging off a cliff high over the valley. If you are more interested in history, you will find your driver or guide pays special attention to show you the important historical sites of the regions you visit. Make sure you talk this over when booking, as arrangements might have to be made if you find yourself straying from the usual path. Your hotel can help you book a tour, or you can speak to the company below, who has received high recommendations (including from the writer of this guide).

Make a stop in Ravello, a town as beautiful as its name suggests, which is the highest town you will find on the coast. Bring your camera – you will want to take pictures of the beautiful scenery you see from here. You will also pass by Amalfi, the namesake city of the region, whose beaches and waterfront are the stuff of paintings and songs. You might also want to take a pause in Positano, the town that was so popular with writers and artists in the middle of the last century. Take a stroll around, and take a look at the beautifully colored buildings and houses in this quiet, sleepy town. If you book with your tour company ahead of time, you might even want to stop for lunch in this idyllic town.

Check out this company, and write them about deals they might have when you're visiting.
http://www.benvenutolimos.com/

Pompeii Historical Site

There are no words to describe what it feels like to walk through a city like Pompeii. Despite the empty brothels, houses, temples, and plasters of humans, caught at the moment of their demise, there is something, a feeling in this city that is absolutely impossible to describe. It still lives, empty, hollow, yet filled with shadows of the people that once called this once bustling seaside town home. Pompeii might be one of the most powerful historical sites you will visit on your trip.

You can easily take the train, if you do not want to go with a private tour, to Pompeii. It's a 30-40 minute journey from Sorrento (disembark at Pompeii Scavi.) Once you get off the train, you will find the entrance to Pompeii a few minutes up the road, past souvenir trucks and snack stands. You may want to buy a bottle of water there. It will be fairly pricey, but there will be nothing once you get inside the actual ruins. It costs 11 Euros for a full-day pass.

The history of Pompeii is tragic. In around 200 BC, the Romans took over Pompeii, and the town was under Roman rule until its demise on August 24th, 79. When Vesuvius erupted, Pompeii was a bustling town, with markets, shops, and more than its share of brothels to attract the sailors to the city. The merchants were rich and corpulent, and the women beautiful. When Vesuvius erupted, 20,000 people were stopped in their tracks, and killed on the spot.

You can still see the remains of many people killed almost 2,000 years ago, the expressions on their faces as if they died yesterday. Women cower over their babies, men reach out to protect their wives. Pompeii is a city stuck in time, and with the techniques of modern-day excavation, mostly free to wander and explore. It is much larger than you expect, so bring your walking shoes, and an extra bottle of water. Also, explore the history of Pompeii before you arrive, so you can choose the sites you want to see on your journey. Sights to see include:

The Amphitheater – this hearkens back to the time of gladiators and deadly combat. It is wonderfully preserved.

The House of the Vetti – you want to visit this site for the plethora of multi-colored frescoes. They each tell a story, and you won't want to miss the fresco of the God of Fertility.

The Temple of Apollo – this is a site in Pompeii where you can see artifacts dating from even before the Romans took over, back to the Etruscan time.

Take a look at the website (click on the British flag for the English version) for directions, times, and rates. http://www.pompeiturismo.it/index.php?Itemid=28&id=14&option=com_content&task=view&lang=en

Capri Island

Take a short boat trip out to the island of Capri, and it will be no surprise to you why many celebrities (including Mariah Carey) like to call this little island their home away from home. Capri is in the Gulf of Naples, on the south side, and has been a resort for over 2,000 years. One step on this island and you'll know why people have been coming here for more than two millennia, and why even Napoleon tried to take over the island. You would want to, too.

There are two main cities on Capri. The cities are Capri (with more than 7,000 inhabitants), and Anacapri (about 6,000 inhabitants). If those aren't numbers enough for you, then how about this: 2 million. That's the amount of people who visit Capri each year. It is only 25 minutes from Sorrento, and 50 minutes from Naples by boat, so it's no wonder so many people flock to this gorgeous island on a romantic and beautiful getaway each year.

There are so many things to see and do during your trip to Capri, you may want to stay the night. But a good place to start is with a boat tour around the island, to get a sense of its tiny size, and also a close-up glimpse of the crystal clear waters around the island. A few things you will see include La Grotta Azzurra (the blue grotto), possibly one of the most famous grottoes in the world. If you're lucky, the tide will be low and your boat captain will be courageous, and he will slip your boat underneath the cliff to take a look at the grotto, and its glowing blue water, from inside the island. It is a sight not to be forgotten. You might also see the Natural Arch, which is a beautiful natural formation of rock along the side of the island, and you can be reminded of the natural power of the water.

No trip to Capri is complete without a trip to the "Piazzetta", which translates to "the little piazza." There are cafés, restaurants, newsagents, and a tourism office so that you can buy a newspaper or a guide, a coffee or glass of wine, and kick up your heels and join the town in watching the rest of the world go by. It is a gorgeous place to look at the sunset from a little spot behind the town's ex-cathedral, and you might find that you wish sunset were just a little longer, so that you could just take one more picture, have one more glass of wine. But don't fret. After sunset, the town heats up and you'll have more than enough chances to eat and dance your way to nirvana.

Just moments away from the Piazzetta, you might want to pop into Al Grottino on Via Longano, 27 for a meal that you will not forget. Tuck your head underneath the beautiful white archways and vaulted ceilings to tuck yourself into a dinner that is as marvelous to eat as it is to savor. Expect light traditional Mediterranean fare, local wines, and more specialties than is possible to count. Call them at 081 8370584 to see about reservations.

You can find more about the island of Capri at the website: http://www.capri.com/

Naples

About two hours from Sorrento, you will find a day trip unlike any other to Napoli (Naples). Unlike other places in Italy, even the locals will tell you to hold on to your purses here! Naples is a dark, gritty place, with layer upon layer of history, in some places garbage, buildings, and crypts forming the winding streets and hills of Naples. It is a place unlike any other, and is absolutely massive. It's a good idea that before you come here, you plan your day(s) well, as there is much to do, and you may want to book private transportation, as the public transportation sometimes even smells like it hasn't been cleaned in a few centuries.

One of the things you should do on your trip to Naples is the Castel Nuovo. This is a huge castle built in the 13th century that gives you a true glimpse of what life must have been like those hundreds of years ago. Inside are frescoes and paintings, and more historical artifacts than you're going to know what to do with. For a history buff, this is one sight not to miss.

Address: Via Vittorio Emanuele III 80133 Naples, Italy
Telephone: 081 7955877
http://www.comune.napoli.it/flex/cm/pages/ServeBLOB.php/L/EN/IDPagina/1372

Take the Funiculare, or inclined train, up the hill to the Vomero district. This is a district that is very popular in the evening, and is teeming with locals out for an after-dinner stroll and tourists. You will absolutely want to try a Zeppoli, which is fried bread filled with tomato sauce. This will be a perfect way to stave off dinner for just one more stroll, just one more store.

You will want to visit the Duomo in Naples, which was built in the 1200s and is an excellent example of Gothic architecture. It was built and dedicated to Naples' patron saint, San Gennaro, and directly next to it is the 4th century Basilica, which has amazing frescoes and columns.

Address: Via Duomo, Naples, Province of Naples, Italy
Telephone: 081 449097
http://www.duomodinapoli.it/

SORRENTO TRAVEL GUIDE

Recommendations for the Budget Traveller

Places to Stay

There are quite a few places to stay in the region around Sorrento. Your best bet is to do your research before your visit, and decide how many days you'd like to spend in each location. Here are a few places to get you started.

Sorrento

L'Angolo di Paradiso: One option to consider when you stay in Sorrento is to try a hotel in the Agriturismo movement. This movement aims to place visitors in local homes and farms, for a unique and ecologically sound housing option. L'Angolo di Paradiso, located right smack in the middle of Sorrento, is a beautiful farm surrounded by olives, lemons, and oranges. You can open your window and just feel the mixture of the salt water and lemon trees splash up against your face. There are six bedrooms here, as well as a restaurant that serves local and the freshest of fresh food you could possibly imagine. Breakfast is included, as well, so you can stock up for your busy day of touring.

Address: Via Monticelli, 2 c/o Il Corso Italia 333 - Sorrento 80067
http://www.agriturismo.it/en/farmhouse/campania/naples/LAngolodiParadiso-6190811/contact.html

Another good option, but if you want a "standard" hotel room, with no farm in sight, is the Hotel Il Nido, which has decent prices and has a beautiful view of the sea.

Address: Via Nastro Verde, 62 80067 Sorrento, Province of Naples, Italy
Telephone: 081 8782766
http://www.ilnido.it/

Ravello (Amalfi Coast)

Bed and Breakfast I Limoni: This Bed and Breakfast is in Ravello, which is a good place to stay on your tour of the Amalfi Coast. This is up a hill some ways, but is a great budget choice, and is actually part of a farm that produces lemons. Want to bet they make some great limoncello there? Also included is breakfast.

Address: Via Gradoni 14, San Cosma, Ravello
Telephone: 089 858056
www.bb-ilimoni.com

Pompeii

Hotel Apollo Pompeii is a nice, budget hotel located very close to the ruins of the city, so at the end of a long day of dusty walking, you can kick back and relax in your room, or in one of the hotels restaurants.

Address: Via Carlo Alberto 18, Pompeii
Telephone: 081 863 0309
http://www.hotelapollopompei.com/

Naples

Bed and Breakfast Bonapace Porta Nolana:

This is close to the central station of Naples, so you can arrive then directly afterwards kick off your shoes and unpack. This is a clean, cheap option for those of you wanting to stay in the center of city, which has easy access to the port for trips to Capri, or up the hill to the shopping and restaurants in the Vomero District.

Address: Via San Cosmo Fuori Porta Nolana 4 - Naples
Telephone: 877-662-6988
http://www.bonapaceaccomodation.com/

Places to Eat

It is difficult to choose just a few recommendations for where to eat in the Sorrento area. If you're lucky, your guide along the coast of Amalfi will lead you to a restaurant tucked away in the hills, or on a secluded beach somewhere. Here are some tried and true choices for your time in beautiful Sorrento.

Sant'anna da Emilia

Sant'anna da Emilia is a charming place to get a delicious local meal. It is modestly priced, and is actually located in a former boat shed, adding to its historical appeal. Don't expect any pricey or sophisticated meals here; this trattoria is focused on serving fresh, local foods such as spaghetti with mussels or gnocchi, Sorrento-style. Pair your meal with the house wine, red or white, and sit back and enjoy. Reservations are usually not possible, so arrive before you want to eat if you come in tourist season, or be prepared to wait.

Address: Via Marina Grande 62, Sorrento
Telephone: 081 807 2720

Zi'Antonio

Zi'Antonio, which translates to "Uncle Tony" is a great option for those of you wanting to eat in the fishing village of Sorrento. It is small, and quaint, and its tiny size allows for personalized service at modest process. What makes this restaurant special is its private taxi service, which will send a car to your hotel and drive you back again (just make sure to tip the driver). Expect well-cooked local dishes and a long, lazy meal.

Address: Via Luigi De Maio, 11 – 80067, Sorrento
Telephone: 081 8781623
http://www.zintonio.it/

Taverna Azzura

For a lovely place to eat after bathing to your heart's content in Marina Grande, try Taverna Azzura. It's known for its fried squid, a local favorite, and is located right on the water's edge. It is an extremely short walk from Piazza Tasso, and you will find it small but popular, so arrive ready to wait, or sit on the beach with a bottle of beer and await the local delicacies that will be sampling at dinner. A good idea, if you like seafood, is to try the catch of the day, which will always be prepared very lightly; sautéed with butter and garlic, and perhaps some lemon.

Address: 166 Marina Grande, Sorrento
Telephone: 081 877 2510
Website: www.taverna_azzurra.it

Gelateria Davide

No trip to Italy is complete without at least one gelato (ice cream.) One of the best places to sample some gelato on your journey is the Gelateria Davide. He's been in business since 1957, and you'll find this an ideal place to relax after a long day's touring. Try a coffee while you're there, or a sandwich or cake if you're hungry for more than ice cream.

Address: Sorrento Via P.R. Giuliani, 41 - Sorrento
Telephone: 081 8781337
http://www.davideilgelato.com/

Places to Shop

Tourists have been coming to shop on the Amalfi coast for centuries. From pottery to jewelry, to fabrics and fresh produce and fish, there is no shortage of things to open your purse strings for in Sorrento. So if you're a bit sunburnt and tired of the beach, head back into town and check out the following places:

Macramé

Macramé is located a few steps away from the historic Piazza Tazzo, and is a perfect place to look for lady's fashion, including hats, coats, bags, scarves, and gloves. This store has been open for quite some time, so it is fun to think of what famous people have shopped here before you.

Address: Via Luigi De Maio, 28 80067 Sorrento
Telephone: 081 8773114
http://www.sorrentotour.it/macrame/

Limonoro

It would be a sin to come all the way to Sorrento and at least not sample the local liquor, Limoncello. It probably would be just as bad not to come home with some for your friends and family. Head to Limonoro to find all sorts of lemon liquors and sweets, and other local delicacies to either bring back for your loved ones or keep just for yourself.

Address: Via San Cesareo, 49/53 0067 Sorrento
Telephone: 081 8785348
www.limonoro.it

De Cenzo

If you want to go home with some of Sorrento's beautiful ceramics, then look no further than De Cenzo, which specializes in handicrafts such as ceramics and paintings. Even if you don't go home with anything, it is a special treat to walk through the aisles of this store, gazing at crafts that are just as gorgeous as the treasures you could find in a museum.

Address: Via Tasso, 23 80067 Sorrento
Telephone: 081 8784757
www.decenzo.it

SORRENTO TRAVEL GUIDE

Printed in Great Britain
by Amazon.co.uk, Ltd.,
Marston Gate.